I0173147

A NEW BEGINNING

A New Beginning

POETRY BY
BARBARA BLACKMON

A Word From the Author

My name is Barbara Ann Blackmon (Gipson). These poems was born out of my struggles that I faced each day which gave me hope to persevere through my adversities. I hope that as I share my poems with each reader, you would come to know that God will surely bring you through any situation when you put Him first. I don't mean for this to sound like another cliché or meaningless rhetoric; for my Lord has always been there for me, even when I didn't recognize that He gave me these skills to write.

Acknowledgements

I would like to give thanks to Mama Janet Gregory for her faithful support, which helped me develop a "back-bone" to persevere in life; to Vernice Gipson for giving me life; to Dorothy, whom I love dearly; to my most beloved Daddy (who has gone on to be with the Lord), Jewel McCarthy. Thank you all for your support. My love to each of you.

The Philosophy of many is to "live it up: eat, drink and be merry: for tomorrow we die!" Life is so much more than just partying. I am so grateful God has given me an opportunity to reach my goal of becoming a writer. Also letting others know that you can truly do ANYTHING, you set your mind to, If you have Faith (confidence) in God.

Dedication to My Daddy (1949-1998)

I know you're among celestial places looking
down on me. So precious you are to me, yet
more precious to God. I miss you so much
though
you're in a much better place. I want you to know
Daddy, I miss your smiling face.

A Father's Steadfast Love

My father was a good man

A tower of strength for me

Made sure that I was okay.

His love for me... unconditional.

Dad's love never suffered a breakdown... he

was always strong and kind.

No other father can take his place.

Only the Father above can surpass my father's

love.

A New Beginning

If I could change my past, I don't think I would.
I wouldn't change the way I was raised.
Wouldn't change a thing.
May each day be a new beginning for me…a
new adventure and let the past stay the past.
The lessons of life make us stronger…if we let
them. God is doing a new thing in me.
I'll leave the problems in His hands.

A Stranger

I have travelled from one town to another, a
Stranger alone and empty
My destination – no place particular
Stopped at one town where peace was found
Love was shown and happiness around
Think I'll stay awhile...long enough to not be a
stranger.
Visit with the people
Enjoy a little peace of mind and share a smile
No more wandering
A stranger no longer; now a friend

Games vs. True Love

Every relationship will have problems – it's a
packaged deal.
To lead someone on, is a big hit below the belt.
Playing games with someone's emotion should
never be an option.
Leave or stay; should you stay…stay true…stay
faithful
If you want to play a game…play a sport
When it comes to matters of the heart, games
are illegal. To cause hurt because you've been
hurt is selfish and immature. But God so loved
the world that He gave Himself. No games
involved…His love is real…His love is
everlasting.
This is true love

Stand

I made a stand and trusted God

My poetry is a gift from you Lord

Weak in belief at first...now I stand

Learning to be strong in your strength

Can't stand on my own; your right hand holds

me. My poetry was His plan.

Right Thing to Do

I told you that I loved you, you never said it
back. My heart grieved, but I was still glad I
said it. It was the right thing to do.
When we last met, I kissed your forehead.
And I said those words again
It was still the right thing to do.
I smiled and said see you later
You smiled back and Your smile said I love
you. Glad I did the right thing.

Trouble

So much trouble

Seems like my whole world is coming

unwound.

My mind…inundated with confusion

If that's not enough…my enemy is trying to

destroy me.

But Jesus said, "Let not your heart be

troubled…"

WOW Lord, my troubles seem so few, when I

focus on you.

Cry Out

Someone cries out for help...are they heard?
Someone cries out...agonizing over the
absence or loss of a loved one. Someone can
even cry out for joy.
An exclamation.
There are many reasons that we cry out.
Crying is a release and it is the beginning of
healing.
I cry because a burden has been lifted from
me. Cry out of pain, cry out of joy.
Cry out!

1-800-Jesus

Most toll free numbers are a dime a dozen.

But there's a special one...not only for

problems, but for praise as well.

No busy signals...no placements on hold

You don't even have to go through a middle

man; you talk directly to the CEO...

Speak personally to the King of Kings...the

Lord of Lords

Just dial 1-800 Jesus.

24/7

He's just a prayer away

Angel on Assignment

Having a bad day
Everything going crazy...even at the job
Asking God for strength
Suddenly feel His presence
My co-worker (Van) comes in.
And like an angel sent from God
Van's attitude changes my whole situation
His jokes invoke much laughter and enjoyment.
Chaos has diminished.
Van, this poem's for you.
You've been an angel on assignment.
God used you to make a difference.

Watching Over Me

As I look out the window…the trees are
dancing in the wind. The rain casually streaks
across the windows. The thunder roars
fearlessly. I tell myself over and over…how
blessed I am. Through all these things, I see
the power and majesty of God.
For even through the storm, He watches over
me.

BELIEVE

Believe in yourself and have faith in God.
You can make it.
We spend too much time complaining about
things we can't change.
Be thankful for what you have.
Many people wish they had your problems
There's always someone in worse shape than
you. Trust God…He won't overload you with
burdens. Believe in Him and in yourself
He won't give up on you.

Better Days

Even when the sun doesn't shine

Better days will come.

Though endless days of rain

Better days will eventually come.

Every morning when I wake

Is my better day

For it's a new day to trust Him.

Water

Sitting on the river bank
Watching the water flow peacefully
The ducks swim effortlessly.
Serenity.
Hectic events cannot exist here
Togetherness and wholeness abound
The peace of this watery scene, resembles a
peace that surpasses understanding.
Tranquil, peaceful waters
One of God's masterpieces

Without Christ

Controlled by the flesh
Unresolved grief.
Hurt feelings…a normalcy
Anarchy and disorder rule
People turning away from God
Without Christ, these things are routine.
Chaos and tribulations are a part of life
But I can't imagine not having Christ in my life.

Words to Live By

I'm not a motivator

I have problems living by my own words.

And my sister had a point; words to live by

should apply to me first.

Stay strong...keep your head up...when you

fall down, get back up...you plus God is

the majority.

I must listen to my own words.

And learn to live by the words I speak

Work

So many people out of work.

Yet so many complain about their jobs.

Complaining about the boss

Complaining about the pay

Stirring up discord and making others

miserable.

Be grateful for the work you do

Do it as unto the Lord

Don't be part of the problem, be part of the

solution

Does it matter?

Does it matter what color you are?

Does it matter what race you are?

Does it matter what clothes you wear?

It really doesn't matter at all.

God loves you just the way you are.

Color doesn't mean a thing to Him.

People are the same no matter their

Background.

He sees us through His Son.

Don't Give Up

Even though it's hard to achieve my goals, I
don't give up.
Even though my temper is very short, I don't
give up.
Even though I want to quit, I don't give up.
Even though I don't have the best of job, I don't
give up.
Because I know that God is God, I'm never
giving up.

Early Morning

Sitting outside…pondering on how blessed I
am. Listening to the melodious sounds of the
fowls of the air. Imagining outlandish shapes
of each cloud formation. And I realize that
tomorrow is not promised to us. Live for
today…tomorrow will take care of itself.
Bathe in the beauty of this glorious early
morning. Thank you Lord!
The magnificence of this splendid morning is
exquisite.

Hearts and Roses

These symbols Unequivocally are two of my
favorite.
A quote from Shakespeare's Romeo and Juliet
"…that which we call a rose, by any other
name would smell as sweet."
The beauty and aroma of a rose, is as the
fragrance of a life well lived.
Whether it is the smell of a freshly picked rose
Or the bouquet of someone's unselfish heart,
which contains no guile.
Sweetness emits from them both.

In Memory Of My father "Jewell McCarthy"
1949-1998

Since you've been gone,

It gets harder and harder to just go on.

But I hear your voice encouraging me

So I don't give in…I don't give up

"Daddy, your baby is going to be a writer!"

I'm going to accomplish my dreams…my goals.

Your love is deep in my soul.

Still missing you.

It's About Being a Lady

A person can be what they chose to be.

It's all about the way you carry yourself.

The opinion of others doesn't matter

Walk with dignity…integrity

To be respected, you must respect yourself.

I will be myself and be a lady.

Janie's Joy

(This poem is dedicated to a Wonderful Lady)

Janie's Joy

Makes me strong when I'm weak.

Janie's smile

Makes me smile when I'm low.

Your joy is a light to others

Brightening their day

You can't help but feel better

When she's around.

Thank you Janie

For sharing your joy

Just Maybe

It was like a dream to me.

I've always wanted to write

And one day sit next to Maya Angelou

Or write a song for Shirley Caesar.

These two ladies...incredibly exceptional to me

Their achievements

Have helped keep my dreams going.

Just maybe

My words may touch someone to go on with

their dreams.

Just maybe

Keep Your Head Up

Keeping my head up
For many downs will come.
I'm keeping my head up,
I will stay strong!
Won't let you put me down
There's a goal in my view.
Keeping my head up
I will make it through
Dreaming the impossible dream
Reaching the unreachable star

Marriage

God brought you together

No man can separate you.

Express your love for one another

Love is not provoked or puffed up

This is a must to hold a marriage together.

Trust and respect for each other.

Impartial care for one another

The couple that prays together stays together

Me against the World

Have you ever felt like the whole world was
against you?
It can sometimes feel that way
Because life is not fair...but what is?
People are sometimes cruel
Bad things do happen to good people.
But I believe Romans 8:28,
"All things work together for good, for those
who love the Lord."

Caught up in the Moment

Momentarily, I was on a cloud drifting away...oh so tranquil. Another moment, I was a millionaire...extraordinary. In that moment, I was in an alternate dimension. Yes, we all have different moments. Finally, I woke up back in the real world. It was great fading away into the moment.

My Birthday

Another birthday. Thank you Lord!

I look over my life blessings galore

Yes I'm older extra pains

Continued difficulties but no time for self-pity

My best days are still ahead of me!

My Dream

My dream...to be the first in my family to
succeed.

Celebrity status...maybe?

Renown novelist or playwright...one never knowws

Dare to dream

Beat the odds

Welcome challenges

Establish goals

Discipline myself

Oh yes...my dream...to succeed.

My Life

Studying numbers for my new job

Grateful, but not satisfied

Wish I could win the lottery.

Not getting my hopes up too high.

I really am blessed

My life may not be the best,

But it's my best for now.

Personal

Getting older means I get wiser...right?

I should realize I can't change my childhood.

Even an estranged relationship with my mother

(Thankful it was only temporary)

Felt like the only family I had was gone.

In all reality that's not true.

God's Word states that if my mother and father

forsake me,

The Lord will take care of me.

Had to let go of my anger.

Surrendered to the Lord

He knows (and can handle) both of us.

No More

No more words to say

No more letters to write

No more songs to sing

No more tears to cry

No more love to give

Nothing left in me

What's the point in saying I love you

When there's no more of you

Now

Let me smell the flowers now.

Let me walk in the park today.

No more procrastination

Will share my feelings without delay.

So let me feel the wind blowing now.

Let me get to know you now.

Let me enjoy life

And do what I can do…now.

See You Again

Never will I say goodbye
Because I'll see you again.
We have so much to talk about.
Though the enemy thought he destroyed you
God's plan was to bring you home.
Yeah I'll see you again
You're really only sleeping
Waiting for Jesus to say arise.
Until then my friend.
I'll see you again.

Short

In life, we take so many things for granted.

We act like our jobs will always be here.

And we even think our loved ones will always

be around.

In reality…Ain't gonna happen!

Life does not work like that.

The days are short…really.

Cherish each one

Take one day at a time.

Appreciate what you have and those you love

Time is too short.

Pain

The pain…excruciating!

Like a devastating blow to the chest.

I stood there and took it.

Tried to walk away…my feet would not move

Frozen

Petrified by anger

You hurt me

Like I hurt you

The physical pain may go away…but scars can

remain

Mental scars/emotional scars…the real pain

Crying persists

Thousands of tear drops

Oh to be healed

From this pain Can't wait!

To Know Someone

To be with someone Is to know that someone.
To talk to someone Is to listen to them.
To understand someone Is to see someone
One day we'll know as we are known

Games

My feelings…can they be trusted?
I wonder where broken hearts go
games people play I don't understand
They say the words you want to hear
yet do the things to hurt you. I played the fool
going all in …with the most tender part of the
body the *heart* not using the smart part the
mind can't seem to get past an old love even
though it's a new day, yet pain just sets you
back feeling sad and hurt behind a person that
had games on their mind.

God's Recipe

One hour of word

Two cups of patience

Three ounces of "hi"

Gallons of smiles

Add a mix of "good job"

Copious amounts of "please" and "thank you".

Stir it all together equals God's Recipe

served daily.

Look at me now

When I look in the mirror who do I see?
The me I see or the me the world sees?
Oh my, look at me know so many times I
couldn't look at me until I saw me as Gods
sees me. Now I keep my head up and say
hey, look at me now! The me the world sees
can be distorted and the me I see is such a
mess... but I proclaim the me God sees is
forgiven and blessed, gratefully and joyfully.
Look at me now!

God Shows Favor

God uses the most unsuspecting of people
to speak into your life. Where do they come
from? I'm Learning daily that even when I am
wrong God never leaves me. When I'm feeling
my worst and it seems nothing going right yet
God shows favor (and mercy). He uses my
supervisor (Pat) to speak into my life. It baffles
me how he allows God to use him no matter
what rank or position he holds in the company.
He helps me see that no matter how things
may get keep a smile. I am most thankful for
God showing favor and how He uses whom He
chooses.

Sit Back

I sit back…looking

I sit back…listening

I sit back…thinking

I sit back and consider all the things I have

I say things could be worst

In spite of my impulse to jump into things

foolishly it's really okay to just sit back

Then I look and listen and think…I dream

Stormy Clouds

I look up at a stormy sky

One side dark, the other side is clear

I have storms in my life

Sometimes very dark and cloudy

But no storm lasts forever

Even hurricanes have eyes

It's clear and calm in the eye

the sun shines in the eye

though surrounded by the storm

the peace of God can and will keep me, even

in the midst I know my storms won't last

forever. The clouds will move and I will see

another sunny day.

Unspoken words

Sometimes we don't always say what we need
until it's too late. So many people leaving this
world today without knowing how much we love them.
So many unspoken words that we could have
said words like I love you, I need you, I miss you,
I forgive you
So many unspoken words
We say I'll tell them tomorrow or the next day
Never wait until the next day to say what needs
to be said today
For today may be your last day (or theirs).

Closed Doors

When you close your door, you can do what
you want for no one can see you behind a
closed door…right? But can closed doors
keep God out? Maybe not doors of wood or
metal but what about doors of the flesh or The
door to a hardened heart.
God will never force His way through that door.
He can open those doors people may shut in
our faces attempting to deny us of
Opportunities and rights But the closed door of
a hardened heart, Can only be open by the
owner of said heart.
Yet His Love beckons the owner to open that door
God forbid if that door remains closed.

Go For It

Don't let your dreams go unrealized…
Go for it
Don't let the stars that you reach for remain
untouched…
Go for it
Setbacks occur, disappointments are inevitable
Never let an underprivileged circumstance
Dictate the outcome of your destiny
You plus God – this combination is always the
majority..
Go for it!

God's Heart

No one really knows God's Heart.
We read what He's done for others and know
what he has done for us. We may know what
His Word says but do we know His heart? For
His ways are not our ways but mercifully, He
gave me plenty second chances. when I cried,
He tenderly comforted me. We'll never
understand His Heart we'll never comprehend
His Love. His Heart is His Love, all we need to
do is receive Him.

Wishes

Are they merely meant for fairy tales and children's books? Are they probably possibilities or a contemptible waste of time? What type of wishes would you wish for? Would they be for selfish or generous? Endeavors? Fame or fortune...health or prosperity? Prosperity equals wealth...not merely financial, but spiritual, mental and emotional wealth. You know what...it's ok to wish.

A Will and A Way

We all go through our ups and downs,
We sometimes wonder... will we ever come out
of it? Will we survive it?
I've heard that where there is a will there is a
way. The will to hope...the will to believe
Believe that God has not forgotten He's the
light at that seemingly never-ending tunnel.
He's there...He's always been there He didn't
say we wouldn't have to go through
heartaches. But that He WILL bring us
THROUGH every one of them!
He IS the WAY!

Tear Drops

I cry many tears for you
Sorrowful tears
Depressing tears
I have seen many people cry
Do you ever cry? ...never saw you shed tears
Are you ever hurt...do you feel my hurt?
Tears drop slowly...drip-drop-drip-drop
Sometimes they flood like a rushing river
So many tears...yet each one lonely
And you can't understand why.

My Christmas Turnaround Story

It was 1998...when I stopped thinking about
Christmas, because I lost my daddy.
Any man can be a father but it takes a special
man to be a daddy. Each year when
Christmas drew near Apathetic, I was
When does the pain go away?
Oh Mama, when does it stop hurting?
Your mom died so many years ago
How do you stay strong?
Wait! Christmas is not about things
It's about Jesus...how He came to give His life
for all.
Christmas is Christ all year around.
Now Christmas reminds me that I'll see my
daddy again.

Heartaches

Living in this body hurts

The pain of aging...the pain of illness

Headaches...heartaches...it hurts

But the worst pain of all is living without Christ

In spite of all of the devastating pains I've

endured I can't imagine not having Christ in my

life.

Walk With Me

Come take a walk with me (God requests),

Ever step you make with me, I'm always right

there with you.

Every breath you take, I breathed into you.

Every heartache you feel, my Love and my

Word, will always be your shoulder to cry on.

We may pass this way many times, you'll never

be alone. (Remember I said WE!)

Time Out

Take time out from the job's daily grind

Take time out from the crowds, even the kids

Take some time from yourself

Take the time

Just you and your "Maker"

You and your "Creator"

Relax...kick your feet up.

Take time out to say, "thank you Lord! I'm

grateful and I'm truly blessed!"

Thank you Lord...for our time.

Slow Down

Here I go again Lord...

Moving too fast

Always in a hurry

Missed my time with you

Have I neglected another blessing?

Bypassed it again

Concerned about my own agenda

I need to slow down

Realizing that when I move too fast

I often go in the wrong direction

Darkness

Darkness...the absence of light
It appears that the darkness is getting darker
An overwhelming abyss Nietzsche said, "...if
you gaze long into an abyss, the abyss will
gaze back into you."
Frightening...terrifying...depressing, Where is
the light? Any light...even a glimmer
Then I remember God's Word Psalm 119:105,
"Your Word is a lamp to my feet, and a light to
my path ."Lamps don't illuminate the entire
area But they do light up enough of my
surroundings that I may not stumble. We can
never escape all darkness But God has
provided His Light.

God sees and hears me

Father, you know my heart

You know my thoughts

You see me for who I am

You've sustained me and provided help for me

Even help in writing these poems

I see them in bookstores

It's already done.

You've heard my cry

Isn't it GREAT! God knows that I exist!

I'm important to Him (and so are you).

Thank you God for seeing and hearing me.

Nevertheless

Many days when I just showed out all along God
seen this and knew how He was going
to use it for His Glory. I acted so foolish but
nevertheless God still got the glory when I
humble myself and said "I am sorry. Although
many times I cried He called me an
Overcomer. He knows just how to show up
and show out. Nevertheless I give Him
the glory for helping me to complete.

Another Day

Is this going to be another one of those days?

When everyone get on your nerves

Tugging you from all directions at the same

time.

Mondays really get a bad rep...For these days

can happen any day

Be careful longing for Fridays

These days may even occur on the weekend.

Already Met

I always wanted to meet the two ladies that I wrote about in my poems. What I didn't know that they were there all along in a different form like Maya Angelo = Sis.Hall she write plays. Then Shirley Ceaser and Tommy Young West. When you see them the way the world see them they are famous. When you see them how God see them they are blessed. So I have meet them and they are the two ladies I wrote about in the poem called "Just Maybe". Now I know what a maybe can be to me. To meet Maya Angelo and Shirley Ceaser is like a dream for a writer to come true.

My Traveling Prayer for You

May you be safe from road rage drivers

May His angels protect you from those who

ignore stop signs and red lights

Cars pass by consistently

I hope you don't ignore God and pass Him by

He's the best traveling companion we'll ever

have.   Follow His directions!

You also can have A New Beginning!

Poetry by
Barbara Blackmon

Published By

New Life Publishing

2131 N. Collins Suite 433-546

Arlington, Texas 76011

877-532-5547

www.ingramcontent.com/pod-product-compliance
Lightning Source LLC
Chambersburg PA
CBHW060423050426
42449CB00009B/2110